Know Your Rights: Legal Protections for Social Security Beneficiaries against Debt Collectors

Clyde N. Cook, III

 First Edition.

Table Of Contents

Chapter 1: Introduction to Your Rights as a Social Security Beneficiary 6

Chapter 2: Clearing Your Credit of Collection Accounts if You're on Social Security 16

Chapter 3: Strategies for Disputing Collection Accounts for Social Security Recipients 25

Chapter 4: Legal Rights of Social Security Beneficiaries in Debt Collection 34

Chapter 5: Financial Counseling for Seniors on Social Security 46

Chapter 6: Understanding the Impact of Collection Accounts on Social Security Benefits 55

Chapter 7: Resources for Free Credit Repair Services for Seniors 65

Chapter 8: Building Credit After a Collection Account for Social Security Beneficiaries 74

Chapter 9: Using Government Programs to Assist with Credit Repair 85

Chapter 10: The Role of Non-Profit Organizations in Helping Social Security Recipients 96

Chapter 11: Conclusion and Next Steps 109

Chapter 1: Introduction to Your Rights as a Social Security Beneficiary

Understanding Social Security Benefits

Understanding Social Security benefits is crucial for seniors and disabled persons who rely on these payments for their livelihood, especially when facing the pressures of bad credit and debt collection. Social Security provides essential financial support, but understanding the intricacies of these benefits can empower beneficiaries to protect their rights and navigate the complexities of debt collection. Social Security benefits can include retirement benefits, disability benefits, and Supplemental Security Income (SSI), each with specific eligibility requirements and financial implications. Beneficiaries should familiarize themselves with their benefits to ensure they are receiving the full amount to which they are entitled.

When dealing with collection accounts, it is important for Social Security recipients to know that their benefits are generally protected from garnishment by most creditors.

This means that creditors cannot legally take away a portion of your Social Security benefits to satisfy a debt. However, there are exceptions, such as for federal taxes or child support. Understanding these protections can provide peace of mind and allow beneficiaries to focus on addressing their financial situations without the fear of losing their primary source of income.

Moreover, disputing collection accounts is a key strategy for those receiving Social Security benefits. If a collection account appears on your credit report that you believe is invalid or inaccurate, you have the right to dispute it.

The Fair Credit Reporting Act allows consumers to challenge inaccuracies, and agencies must investigate these disputes. Beneficiaries should gather documentation related to their Social Security benefits and any other relevant financial records to support their case. Engaging with credit reporting agencies can ultimately help clear erroneous accounts and improve credit scores, thereby enhancing financial stability. For seniors and disabled persons, financial counseling can be a valuable resource. Many organizations offer free or low-cost financial counseling specifically tailored to the needs of Social Security beneficiaries.

These counselors can help individuals create budgets, understand their credit reports, and develop strategies for managing debt. Additionally, they can provide guidance on government programs and resources designed to assist with credit repair, ensuring that beneficiaries are aware of all available options to improve their financial health.

In conclusion, understanding Social Security benefits is essential for seniors and disabled individuals facing challenges related to bad credit and debt collection. By recognizing their rights, utilizing available resources, and seeking assistance when needed, beneficiaries can work towards clearing their credit of collection accounts and building a more secure financial future. Engaging with non-profit organizations and financial counselors can provide the support necessary to navigate these issues effectively, empowering beneficiaries to reclaim control over their financial well-being.

Overview of Debt Collection Practices

Debt collection practices have evolved over the years, but they often remain a source of stress and confusion for many, particularly seniors and individuals with disabilities who rely on Social Security benefits. Understanding how debt collectors operate is crucial for these individuals, as it equips them with the knowledge to protect their rights and navigate the complexities of debt collection. Debt collectors may use various methods to recover outstanding debts, including phone calls, written notices, and even legal actions. It is essential for Social Security beneficiaries to recognize their rights and the limitations placed on collectors by law.

The Fair Debt Collection Practices Act (FDCPA) serves as a key legal framework governing the actions of debt collectors. This federal law prohibits abusive, deceptive, and unfair practices in the collection of debts. For seniors and disabled persons receiving Social Security, this means they are protected from threats, harassment, and misleading information.

Collectors are also required to provide validation of the debt upon request, allowing individuals to confirm the legitimacy of the claim being made against them. Understanding these protections can empower beneficiaries to challenge aggressive tactics and seek recourse when their rights are violated.

Seniors and disabled individuals on Social Security may find themselves in unique situations when dealing with collection accounts. Given their fixed income, the impact of these debts can be particularly pronounced, affecting their ability to cover essential expenses. It is crucial for them to understand that certain benefits, including Social Security payments, are typically exempt from being garnished by creditors. Additionally, strategies for disputing collection accounts can be particularly beneficial. Beneficiaries have the right to dispute inaccuracies in their credit reports and should not hesitate to utilize this right when faced with incorrect or unverified debts. Financial counseling can play a significant role in helping Social Security recipients manage their debt situations.

Many organizations offer free or low-cost financial counseling services tailored to seniors, providing them with essential tools and strategies for credit repair and management. These services can help beneficiaries develop budgets, understand their credit reports, and create action plans for addressing collection accounts. Furthermore, by utilizing government programs designed to assist with credit repair, individuals can access resources that may lead to improved financial stability.

Finally, non-profit organizations often play a vital part in supporting Social Security beneficiaries dealing with debt collection issues. These organizations can provide education on legal rights, assist with dispute processes, and offer guidance on building credit after a collection account. By connecting with these resources, seniors and disabled persons can gain valuable insights and support that can help them regain control over their financial situations. Understanding the landscape of debt collection practices and available resources can empower beneficiaries to pursue their rights and work towards a healthier financial future.

Importance of Knowing Your Rights

Understanding your rights as a Social Security beneficiary is crucial, especially when facing the challenges of debt collection. As seniors and disabled individuals, you may find yourselves targeted by aggressive debt collectors who may not fully understand the protections afforded to you. Being aware of your legal rights helps you navigate these situations with confidence, ensuring that you are treated fairly and justly. Knowledge of your rights can empower you to stand up against unlawful collection practices and to advocate for yourself effectively. One of the key aspects of knowing your rights is understanding the legal protections specifically designed for Social Security beneficiaries. The Fair Debt Collection Practices Act provides guidelines on how debt collectors must conduct themselves, prohibiting harassment and deceptive practices. Moreover, Social Security benefits are typically exempt from garnishment by creditors.

This means that even if you have outstanding debts, your Social Security income should remain safeguarded, allowing you to maintain your basic living expenses. Familiarizing yourself with these laws can provide peace of mind and a clear framework for addressing any collection threats you may encounter.

When you are aware of your rights, you can employ effective strategies for disputing collection accounts that may be inaccurately reported on your credit report. If a debt collector contacts you regarding a collection that you believe is erroneous, you have the right to request validation of the debt. This process requires the collector to provide proof that you owe the money they are attempting to collect. Knowing how to challenge these claims not only helps clear your credit report but also protects you from paying debts that are not legitimately yours.

Financial counseling can also play a pivotal role in understanding and exercising your rights. Many non-profit organizations offer free or low-cost credit counseling services specifically tailored to seniors and Social Security recipients.

These resources can guide you through the complexities of your financial situation, helping you develop a plan to address debts while safeguarding your Social Security benefits. Engaging with a financial counselor can provide clarity and direction, ensuring you are leveraging all available options for credit repair and financial stability.

Ultimately, knowing your rights equips you with the tools necessary to rebuild your credit after a collection account. By understanding government programs and community resources available to assist with credit repair, you can take proactive steps towards improving your financial health. Whether it's accessing free credit repair services or learning about government initiatives designed to support Social Security beneficiaries, being informed is the first step toward reclaiming your financial future. Empowerment through knowledge not only benefits you today but also lays the groundwork for a more secure tomorrow.

Chapter 2: Clearing Your Credit of Collection Accounts if You're on Social Security

The Impact of Collection Accounts on Your Credit Score

Collection accounts can significantly impact your credit score, which is a crucial aspect of financial health, especially for seniors and disabled individuals relying on Social Security benefits. When a debt is sent to collections, it indicates to credit bureaus that the account holder has failed to meet their financial obligations. This negative mark can lower your credit score, making it more challenging to obtain loans, secure housing, or even qualify for certain services. Understanding how collection accounts affect your credit is the first step toward regaining control over your financial situation.

For Social Security beneficiaries, the implications of having a low credit score can be particularly severe. Many individuals in this demographic may already face financial constraints, making it difficult to manage outstanding debts. The presence of collection accounts can exacerbate these issues, as potential lenders may view you as a higher risk. This can lead to higher interest rates on loans or even outright denials for credit applications. It is essential to recognize that maintaining a healthier credit score can open doors to better financial opportunities, including access to necessary resources and services.

Seniors and disabled persons should be aware that they have legal rights when it comes to dealing with debt collectors. The Fair Debt Collection Practices Act protects consumers from abusive practices and provides guidelines for how collectors can operate. For instance, you have the right to dispute any collection account that you believe is inaccurate or unfair.

Taking action to dispute these accounts can potentially remove them from your credit report, leading to an improved score. Understanding these rights is crucial for empowering yourself in interactions with debt collectors.

In addition to disputing inaccurate accounts, there are various strategies that can help you manage and clear collection accounts if you are receiving Social Security. Seeking financial counseling can be an effective way to explore your options. Many non-profit organizations offer free or low-cost credit repair services specifically designed to assist seniors and disabled individuals. These resources can provide valuable guidance on budgeting, negotiating with creditors, and developing a plan to improve your credit score over time. Utilizing these services can help alleviate some of the stress associated with debt management. Lastly, rebuilding credit after a collection account is not only possible but can also be a realistic goal for Social Security beneficiaries. Engaging with government programs aimed at assisting low-income individuals can provide additional support in repairing credit.

Programs may offer financial education, assistance in negotiating with creditors, or even direct support in paying off debts. By taking advantage of these resources and understanding your rights, you can work towards a more stable financial future, ensuring that your credit score reflects your efforts and improving your overall quality of life.

Steps to Dispute Inaccurate Collection Accounts

To dispute inaccurate collection accounts, the first step is to gather all relevant documentation. This includes any correspondence you have received from the debt collector, along with your own records that support your claim. For Social Security beneficiaries, it is crucial to review your Social Security statements and any payment records related to medical bills or other debts. This comprehensive documentation will serve as the foundation for your dispute and help you present a factual case.

Once you have compiled your documents, the next step is to contact the credit reporting agencies. Under the Fair Credit Reporting Act, you have the right to dispute any information you believe is inaccurate. You can initiate a dispute with the major credit bureaus—Experian, TransUnion, and Equifax—either online, by mail, or over the phone. When submitting your dispute, include a detailed explanation of why you believe the collection account is inaccurate, along with copies of your supporting documents. Remember to keep copies of everything you send for your records.

After filing your dispute, the credit reporting agency is required to investigate your claim, typically within 30 days. During this period, it is essential to monitor your credit report closely and remain in contact with the agency if necessary. If the agency finds that the information is indeed inaccurate, they are obligated to correct your credit report and inform you of the changes. However, if they uphold the accuracy of the collection account, you still have further options to pursue your case.

If the credit reporting agency does not resolve your dispute favorably, consider reaching out directly to the debt collector. Write a formal letter disputing the debt, clearly stating the reasons for your dispute and referencing any relevant documentation. Under the Fair Debt Collection Practices Act, you have the right to request verification of the debt. If the collector cannot provide sufficient evidence, they are required to cease collection efforts. This step can help protect your rights and provide additional leverage in clearing your credit.

Finally, it is wise to seek assistance from non-profit organizations or financial counseling services that specialize in helping seniors and disabled persons navigate debt-related issues. These organizations can provide valuable resources, support, and guidance as you work to dispute inaccurate collection accounts. Additionally, they may offer free credit repair services or connect you with government programs designed to assist Social Security beneficiaries in improving their credit. Taking these proactive steps can empower you to reclaim your financial health and ensure your credit report accurately reflects your situation.

Removing Collection Accounts from Your Credit Report

Removing collection accounts from your credit report is a crucial step for seniors and disabled persons receiving Social Security benefits. Many individuals in this demographic may find themselves facing collection accounts due to medical expenses, living costs, or other unforeseen financial burdens. It is essential to understand that having collection accounts on your credit report can significantly impact your credit score, making it more challenging to secure loans or credit in the future. Fortunately, there are legal protections and strategies available to help you dispute these accounts and improve your credit standing.

The Fair Debt Collection Practices Act (FDCPA) provides legal rights to consumers, including Social Security beneficiaries, against unfair debt collection practices. If you believe a collection account on your credit report is inaccurate or invalid, you have the right to dispute it. Start by obtaining a copy of your credit report from the three major credit bureaus.

Carefully review the report to identify any collection accounts that may be erroneous or outdated. Once you have pinpointed these accounts, you can file a dispute with the credit bureau, providing evidence to support your claim. The bureau is then obligated to investigate the dispute, which can lead to the removal of the collection account if found to be inaccurate.

In addition to disputing inaccuracies with credit bureaus, it is crucial to communicate directly with the debt collector. Under the FDCPA, you can request validation of the debt, which requires the collector to provide proof that you owe the debt and that they have the right to collect it. If the collector fails to respond or cannot validate the debt, you can demand that they cease all collection efforts. This action can help in the removal of the collection account from your credit report, especially if the debt is not legally enforceable. Seeking financial counseling can also be beneficial for seniors on Social Security facing collection accounts. Many non-profit organizations offer free or low-cost credit counseling services tailored to the needs of older adults and individuals with disabilities.

These organizations can help you understand your rights, develop a budget, and create a plan to manage or eliminate your debts. They can also assist you in navigating the complexities of credit repair and may provide resources to address collection accounts effectively.

Finally, rebuilding your credit after a collection account is possible and essential for financial stability. Once collection accounts are removed, or if you have settled them, focus on establishing positive credit habits. This may include making timely payments on any remaining debts, utilizing secured credit cards, or becoming an authorized user on a trusted friend or family member's credit account. By taking these steps, Social Security beneficiaries can work towards improving their credit scores and achieving better financial outcomes, ultimately leading to a more secure and independent life.

Chapter 3: Strategies for Disputing Collection Accounts for Social Security Recipients

Gathering Documentation for Your Dispute

Gathering documentation is a crucial step in disputing collection accounts, especially for seniors and disabled individuals receiving Social Security. When faced with a collection account, it is essential to collect all relevant information that supports your case. Start by obtaining copies of your credit report from the major credit bureaus - Equifax, Experian, and TransUnion. You are entitled to one free report from each bureau annually. Review these reports carefully to identify any inaccuracies or unfamiliar accounts that may have been reported incorrectly. Keep a record of your findings, as this will serve as the foundation for your dispute.

Next, compile any correspondence you have received from the debt collector. This includes letters, notices, or any other communication regarding the debt. It is vital to note the dates of these communications and any specific details mentioned about the debt, such as the amount owed and the original creditor. If you have made any payments or have any agreements regarding the debt, gather documentation that reflects these transactions. This evidence can be crucial in establishing your case and demonstrating any discrepancies in the collector's claims.

In addition to your credit report and correspondence, gather any documents that verify your income and benefits. This includes Social Security benefit statements, bank statements, and any other records that showcase your financial situation. Demonstrating your reliance on Social Security can help you argue that the collection account is impacting your ability to maintain financial stability. If you have received any financial counseling, collect documentation that outlines your situation and any advice provided, as this can further strengthen your position.

It is also beneficial to gather any legal documents related to the debt, such as court judgments or previous collection attempts. If you have filed complaints with consumer protection agencies or contacted legal aid organizations, keep records of these interactions as well. Having a comprehensive set of documents will not only support your dispute but also provide you with a clearer picture of your rights and options moving forward.

Finally, consider reaching out to non-profit organizations that specialize in assisting Social Security beneficiaries with credit issues. These organizations can provide additional resources and guidance on gathering your documentation and disputing collection accounts. Many offer free services that can help you navigate the complexities of debt collection and advocate for your rights. By ensuring you have all relevant documentation and support, you empower yourself to challenge any inaccuracies on your credit report effectively.

Writing Effective Dispute Letters

Writing effective dispute letters is an essential skill for seniors and disabled persons receiving Social Security, particularly when dealing with collection accounts that can adversely affect their credit. A well-crafted dispute letter serves as a formal notification to debt collectors, asserting your rights and outlining the reasons why the alleged debt may be inaccurate or invalid. It's important to remember that under the Fair Debt Collection Practices Act, you have the right to dispute any debt that you believe is not yours or is being collected incorrectly. This subchapter will guide you through the process of writing an effective dispute letter, ensuring that your rights are upheld.

When beginning your dispute letter, it is crucial to include your personal information at the top, such as your name, address, and contact information. This helps the debt collector easily identify your account. Following this, clearly state the date of the letter and the name of the debt collector you are addressing.

In your opening paragraph, mention the purpose of your letter: to formally dispute the validity of the debt. Be concise and direct, as clarity is key in ensuring that your message is understood.

In the body of your letter, provide specific information about the debt you are disputing, including the account number and the amount you are being asked to pay. If applicable, mention any discrepancies you have noticed, such as incorrect amounts, dates, or even the legitimacy of the debt itself. Supporting your claims with relevant documentation can strengthen your case. For example, if you have proof that you have already settled the debt or that it was never yours in the first place, include copies of these documents with your letter. This evidence can significantly bolster your position.

It is also vital to invoke your rights under the Fair Debt Collection Practices Act. This includes your right to request validation of the debt, which obligates the collector to provide proof that you owe the amount they claim.

Make sure to specify that you are requesting this validation in your letter. Additionally, you can ask the collector to cease communication with you until they provide this proof. This not only protects you from further harassment but also puts the onus on the collector to validate their claim before pursuing any further action.

Finally, always remember to keep a copy of your dispute letter and any enclosures for your records, and send the letter via certified mail with a return receipt requested. This gives you proof of delivery, which may be beneficial if the situation escalates. Writing effective dispute letters is not just about asserting your rights; it is also about taking control of your financial situation. By being proactive and organized in your approach, you can significantly impact how collection accounts affect your credit and, ultimately, your Social Security benefits.

Following Up on Your Dispute

Following up on your dispute with a debt collector is a crucial step in ensuring that your rights as a Social Security beneficiary are upheld. Once you have initiated a dispute regarding a collection account, it is important to keep track of all communications and responses. Documenting every interaction can provide you with a clear record should further action be necessary. This includes noting the date, time, and the names of individuals you speak with, as well as the content of your conversations. Keeping these records will help you maintain a strong case if you need to escalate the matter.

After submitting your dispute, the debt collector is required by law to investigate your claim. This process can take some time, but it is important to follow up if you do not receive a response within a reasonable timeframe. Sending a follow-up letter to the collector, referencing your original dispute, can serve as a reminder of your request and demonstrate your determination to resolve the issue. In your letter, ensure you reiterate the key points of your dispute and request a timeline for when you can expect a resolution.

If the debt collector responds to your dispute, carefully review their findings. Sometimes, collectors may dismiss your dispute without proper justification. If you believe their response is unsatisfactory or if they fail to provide adequate evidence of the debt, you have the right to challenge their findings. You can do this by sending a follow-up letter outlining your reasons for disputing their conclusion and requesting further verification of the debt. It is essential to assert your rights firmly and ensure that you are not held liable for debts that are incorrect or unverifiable.

In addition to direct follow-ups with the debt collector, you should also consider reaching out to credit reporting agencies if the disputed account continues to affect your credit report negatively. Under the Fair Credit Reporting Act, you have the right to dispute information on your credit report if it is inaccurate or incomplete. When doing so, provide the agencies with your dispute documentation and any correspondence with the debt collector. This can help ensure that your credit report accurately reflects your financial situation, which is particularly vital for Social Security beneficiaries who may face unique challenges related to their credit.

Lastly, take advantage of available resources to assist you in navigating the dispute process and improving your credit standing. Non-profit organizations and legal aid services can offer valuable guidance tailored to seniors and disabled individuals receiving Social Security. These resources often provide free financial counseling and can help you understand your rights in the context of debt collection. Engaging with these services can empower you to make informed decisions and build a more secure financial future despite the challenges posed by collection accounts.

Chapter 4: Legal Rights of Social Security Beneficiaries in Debt Collection

The Fair Debt Collection Practices Act

The Fair Debt Collection Practices Act (FDCPA) is a vital piece of legislation that offers protections to individuals against abusive debt collection practices. This law applies not only to the general public but also specifically benefits seniors and disabled persons receiving Social Security. Under the FDCPA, debt collectors are prohibited from using deceptive or harassing tactics to collect debts. This means that if you are receiving Social Security and find yourself facing aggressive collection efforts, you have legal recourse to defend yourself and your rights.

One of the key provisions of the FDCPA is the requirement for debt collectors to provide written validation of the debt they claim you owe.

This validation must include details such as the amount of the debt and the name of the creditor. For Social Security beneficiaries, this is an important protection, as it allows you to verify whether the debt is legitimate or if it may be a mistake. If you believe the debt is inaccurate or if you do not recognize it, the FDCPA allows you to dispute it formally, and the debt collector must cease collection activities until the dispute is resolved.

Seniors and disabled individuals often face unique challenges when it comes to debt collection. The FDCPA recognizes this by ensuring that collectors cannot contact you at inconvenient times or places. For instance, contacting you at your workplace or late at night is prohibited. Additionally, if you request that a collector stop contacting you, they must comply. Understanding these rights can empower Social Security recipients to take control of potentially distressing situations and seek assistance when needed.

In addition to the protections from harassment and the requirement for debt validation, the FDCPA also allows for potential legal action against collectors who violate its provisions.

If a debt collector engages in illegal practices, such as threatening behavior or misinformation, you may have grounds for a lawsuit. This is particularly significant for Social Security beneficiaries who may rely on their limited income and cannot afford to pay debts that are incorrectly pursued. Knowing this can provide peace of mind and encourage you to stand up against unfair practices.

Finally, while the FDCPA offers robust protections, it is also essential to seek additional resources that can assist you in managing debt and improving your credit. Many non-profit organizations and government programs are available to provide financial counseling specifically tailored for seniors and disabled persons. These resources can help you develop strategies for disputing collection accounts, repairing your credit, and building a stronger financial future. Utilizing these services, in conjunction with the protections offered by the FDCPA, can significantly enhance your ability to navigate the challenges of debt collection while receiving Social Security benefits.

Exemptions for Social Security Income

Exemptions for Social Security Income play a crucial role in protecting the financial well-being of seniors and disabled individuals who rely on these benefits. Social Security Income (SSI) is designed to provide essential support for those with limited resources, and as such, it is often exempt from being seized by debt collectors. This legal protection means that creditors cannot garnish SSI benefits for the repayment of debts, allowing beneficiaries to maintain their basic living standards without the fear of losing their primary source of income. Understanding these exemptions is vital for individuals facing financial challenges, particularly when dealing with collection accounts.

When it comes to debt collection, it's important for Social Security beneficiaries to be aware that their income is generally protected under federal law.

The Social Security Administration stipulates that benefits received from SSI are not subject to attachment or garnishment, which means that creditors cannot legally access these funds. This exemption is particularly beneficial for those who may find themselves struggling with bad credit or financial difficulties, as it ensures that a portion of their income remains intact for essential expenses such as housing, food, and medical care.

Additionally, beneficiaries should be informed about the specific procedures in place for disputing collection accounts that may arise. If a collection agency attempts to collect on a debt that they believe is valid, Social Security recipients have the right to dispute the debt if they think it is inaccurate or unfair. This process typically involves sending a written dispute to the collector, which can initiate a review of the account. By understanding these legal rights, beneficiaries can take proactive steps to protect their financial interests and ensure that their Social Security Income remains unaffected by erroneous or illegitimate collection efforts.

For seniors and disabled persons navigating these challenges, financial counseling can provide valuable support. Many organizations offer free or low-cost services tailored to the unique needs of Social Security recipients. These resources can offer guidance on managing debt, understanding credit reports, and developing strategies for improving credit scores. Engaging with a financial counselor can empower individuals to take control of their finances, explore potential government programs for credit repair, and work towards building a more secure financial future.

Furthermore, non-profit organizations play an essential role in assisting Social Security beneficiaries with credit repair and financial literacy. They often provide workshops, one-on-one counseling, and access to legal resources that can help individuals understand their rights and options when dealing with collection accounts. By leveraging these resources, seniors and disabled persons can not only safeguard their Social Security Income but also take meaningful steps towards improving their overall financial situation, ensuring that their benefits are used effectively and protected from unnecessary encroachment by creditors.

Legal Protections Against Harassment

Legal protections against harassment are crucial for seniors and disabled persons receiving Social Security benefits, particularly those dealing with the stress of bad credit and debt collection. The Fair Debt Collection Practices Act (FDCPA) provides a framework designed to protect consumers from abusive debt collection practices. Under this law, debt collectors are prohibited from engaging in harassment, which includes making threatening phone calls, using obscene language, or contacting individuals at unreasonable hours. Understanding these protections can empower Social Security beneficiaries to recognize their rights and take action against inappropriate conduct from debt collectors.

Seniors and disabled individuals who receive Social Security benefits often face unique challenges when it comes to debt collection. There are specific provisions within the FDCPA that recognize the vulnerability of these groups.

For example, collectors cannot disclose details of the debt to third parties without the consumer's consent, which is especially important for individuals who may be living in assisted facilities or have caregivers managing their affairs. Knowing these rights can help beneficiaries maintain their privacy and dignity when dealing with debt collectors.

If a debt collector violates the protections outlined in the FDCPA, individuals have several recourse options. They can file a complaint with the Consumer Financial Protection Bureau (CFPB) or the Federal Trade Commission (FTC), which can investigate and take action against abusive practices. Additionally, individuals may consider seeking legal advice from attorneys who specialize in consumer rights. Many of these professionals offer free consultations, allowing beneficiaries to understand their options without incurring financial strain, which can be particularly beneficial for those on fixed incomes.

It is also essential to understand the potential impact of collection accounts on Social Security benefits.

In many cases, Social Security payments cannot be garnished for debts, providing a layer of protection for beneficiaries. However, if a collection account negatively affects an individual's credit score, it might limit their access to necessary loans or financial assistance. Seniors and disabled individuals should be aware that while they have legal protections against harassment, they also have the right to dispute inaccurate collection accounts, ensuring their financial records accurately reflect their circumstances.

Finally, various resources are available to assist Social Security beneficiaries in navigating debt collection issues and improving their credit. Non-profit organizations often provide free financial counseling, helping individuals create budgets, understand their rights, and develop strategies to manage debt. Additionally, government programs may offer assistance in repairing credit or connecting beneficiaries with legitimate credit repair services. By utilizing these resources, seniors and disabled persons can empower themselves to advocate for their rights and work towards financial stability, ultimately enhancing their quality of life.

Chapter 5: Financial Counseling for Seniors on Social Security

Finding the Right Financial Counselor

Finding the right financial counselor can significantly impact the financial well-being of seniors and disabled persons receiving Social Security. When faced with bad credit and the stress of debt collection, it is essential to seek guidance from professionals who understand the unique challenges faced by Social Security beneficiaries. A qualified financial counselor can provide personalized advice, help develop a realistic budget, and create a plan to address outstanding debts while safeguarding your Social Security benefits.

To begin the search for a suitable financial counselor, it is crucial to look for professionals with specific experience in working with seniors and those on fixed incomes.

Many counselors offer services tailored to the needs of individuals facing financial hardships due to medical expenses, reduced income, or unexpected life changes. Checking credentials and affiliations with reputable organizations, such as the National Foundation for Credit Counseling, can also be beneficial. This ensures that the counselor adheres to ethical standards and provides trustworthy services.

Another important consideration when selecting a financial counselor is the approach they take towards debt management. Some counselors may focus on debt settlement, while others emphasize budgeting and credit rebuilding strategies. It is vital to choose a counselor who respects your rights as a Social Security beneficiary and understands how collection accounts can affect your benefits. Discussing their methods and asking for examples of how they have helped clients in similar situations can provide insight into their effectiveness and compatibility with your financial goals.

Affordability is a significant concern for many Social Security recipients. When seeking financial counseling, inquire about the fees involved and whether they offer sliding scale options based on income. Some non-profit organizations provide free or low-cost financial counseling services, making them accessible to individuals with limited resources. Additionally, look for counselors who offer pro bono services or are affiliated with community organizations that support seniors and disabled persons, ensuring you receive assistance without adding further financial strain.

Finally, trust and comfort are essential components of the counseling relationship. You should feel safe discussing your financial situation openly and honestly. A good financial counselor will listen to your concerns, validate your feelings, and work collaboratively with you to develop a tailored plan. Building a relationship with a counselor who demonstrates empathy and understanding will empower you to take control of your financial future, paving the way for improved credit and stability in your Social Security benefits.

Understanding Budgeting and Debt Management

Understanding budgeting and debt management is crucial for seniors and disabled persons receiving Social Security benefits, especially when grappling with bad credit. Effective budgeting allows individuals to allocate their limited resources wisely, ensuring that essential expenses such as housing, healthcare, and food are prioritized. By creating a detailed budget that outlines monthly income and expenditures, beneficiaries can gain a clearer understanding of their financial situation, which is the first step toward managing debt effectively. This process can help identify areas where costs can be reduced, making it easier to navigate financial obligations and plan for the future.

When it comes to debt management, it is essential to recognize the legal protections available to Social Security beneficiaries. The Fair Debt Collection Practices Act provides guidelines that debt collectors must follow, ensuring that they do not engage in abusive or harassing behavior.

Understanding these rights can empower recipients to address collection attempts with confidence. Additionally, Social Security benefits are generally exempt from garnishment for most types of debts, meaning that these funds cannot be seized to pay off existing liabilities. This protection allows individuals to focus on budgeting and managing their finances without the constant threat of losing their primary source of income.

For those dealing with collection accounts, disputing inaccuracies on credit reports is a vital strategy. Social Security recipients should regularly review their credit reports for errors that may negatively impact their scores. If a collection account appears that is inaccurate or should not be there, individuals have the right to dispute it with the credit bureau. Proper documentation and a clear explanation of the dispute can lead to the removal of erroneous items, thereby improving credit scores over time. Utilizing the resources available through government programs and non-profit organizations can also provide assistance in navigating these disputes effectively.

Financial counseling can play a significant role in helping seniors on Social Security develop better budgeting and debt management practices. Many organizations offer free or low-cost financial counseling services specifically designed for vulnerable populations. These counseling sessions can provide personalized advice on creating budgets, managing debts, and building credit after a collection account. For Social Security beneficiaries, seeking out these resources can lead to improved financial literacy and greater control over their financial circumstances.

Lastly, understanding the long-term impact of collection accounts on Social Security benefits is essential. While collection accounts can affect credit scores, they do not directly influence Social Security benefits. However, the stress and anxiety associated with debt can impact overall well-being, which is why it is vital to address these financial issues proactively. By utilizing available resources, including government programs and non-profit organizations dedicated to helping Social Security recipients, individuals can work towards repairing their credit and improving their financial health.

Ultimately, effective budgeting and debt management are key components in achieving financial stability and peace of mind for seniors and disabled persons living on Social Security.

Resources for Financial Education

Accessing reliable resources for financial education is crucial for seniors and disabled individuals receiving Social Security, especially those grappling with bad credit. These resources can empower beneficiaries by providing the knowledge and tools necessary to navigate the complexities of debt collection and improve their financial standing. Understanding where to find credible information is the first step toward regaining control over one's financial situation.

One valuable resource is the Consumer Financial Protection Bureau (CFPB), which offers a wealth of information tailored for consumers struggling with debt. Their website features guides on disputing debts, understanding credit scores, and knowing your rights in the debt collection process.

Seniors can benefit from the CFPB's specialized resources, which are designed to be easily comprehensible and applicable to their unique circumstances. Additionally, the CFPB provides sample letters for disputing collection accounts, helping Social Security recipients assert their rights effectively.

Local community organizations often provide free financial counseling services specifically aimed at seniors and individuals with disabilities. These non-profit organizations can assist with budgeting, managing debt, and understanding credit reports. Many have programs tailored to the needs of Social Security beneficiaries, offering personalized advice that takes into account their fixed incomes and specific challenges. By connecting with these organizations, individuals can receive one-on-one support and develop actionable strategies to improve their financial health.

Moreover, various government programs are available to assist Social Security recipients with credit repair. The Department of Housing and Urban Development (HUD) offers resources for housing-related financial issues, including credit counseling.

Additionally, the Social Security Administration provides information on how debt can affect benefits, guiding recipients on how to protect their income from collection actions. Utilizing these programs can provide seniors with additional avenues to address their credit issues while safeguarding their essential benefits.

Finally, online platforms and community workshops focused on financial literacy can serve as excellent supplementary resources. Many libraries and community centers host free classes on credit repair, budgeting, and debt management. These sessions often feature experts who can answer questions and provide guidance specific to the needs of seniors and disabled individuals. By taking advantage of these educational opportunities, Social Security beneficiaries can enhance their understanding of financial management, empower themselves against debt collectors, and work toward a more secure financial future.

Chapter 6: Understanding the Impact of Collection Accounts on Social Security Benefits

How Collection Accounts Affect Your Benefits

Collection accounts can have a significant impact on the financial well-being of seniors and disabled persons receiving Social Security. When a debt goes unpaid for an extended period, it may be sent to a collection agency, resulting in a negative mark on your credit report. This can lead to a lower credit score, making it harder to secure loans or obtain favorable interest rates. For Social Security beneficiaries, this situation can be particularly challenging. Many rely on fixed incomes, making it essential to maintain good credit to ensure access to necessary resources, such as housing and medical care.

Understanding your legal rights in the context of debt collection is crucial for protecting your benefits. The Fair Debt Collection Practices Act (FDCPA) offers legal protections against harassment and abusive practices by debt collectors. Social Security payments are generally exempt from garnishment, meaning that creditors cannot take these benefits to satisfy a debt. However, it is important to remain informed about your rights and take action if you believe that a collector is violating those rights. Documenting any communication and seeking legal advice can empower you in disputes.

Disputing collection accounts can be a viable strategy for improving your credit profile. If you believe that a collection account is inaccurate or does not belong to you, you have the right to dispute it with the credit bureaus. Provide documentation that supports your claim, such as records of payments or correspondence with the original creditor. Additionally, consider reaching out to the collection agency to negotiate a settlement or payment plan. Many collectors are willing to work with you, especially if you can demonstrate a genuine inability to pay in full.

Financial counseling services can provide invaluable assistance for seniors on Social Security dealing with collection accounts. Non-profit organizations often offer free or low-cost counseling to help you understand your financial situation and develop a plan to manage your debt. These resources can help you create a budget, prioritize debts, and explore options for credit repair. Taking advantage of these services can lead to better financial management and improved credit, ultimately enhancing your quality of life.

Finally, government programs and non-profit organizations play a vital role in assisting Social Security recipients in credit repair efforts. Many local and national programs are designed to help individuals understand their credit rights and provide tools for rebuilding credit after facing collection accounts. These resources often include workshops, one-on-one counseling, and access to credit repair services. Engaging with such programs can empower you to take control of your financial future and strengthen your position as a Social Security beneficiary, ensuring that you have the support needed to navigate the complexities of debt collection.

The Relationship Between Credit and Financial Security

The relationship between credit and financial security is particularly significant for seniors and disabled individuals who rely on Social Security benefits. For many in this demographic, a negative credit history can create barriers to accessing essential services, securing affordable housing, and navigating daily expenses. Understanding how credit scores affect financial security is crucial for those who may feel overwhelmed by debt collection practices and the challenges of managing their financial situations on a fixed income. Awareness of their rights and resources can empower Social Security beneficiaries to take control of their credit health, leading to greater financial stability.

Collection accounts can have a profound impact on the credit scores of Social Security recipients. A lower credit score may lead to higher interest rates on loans or even denial of credit altogether, making it more difficult to recover from financial setbacks.

Moreover, collection accounts can remain on a credit report for up to seven years, limiting opportunities for improvement. It is essential for beneficiaries to understand the implications of these accounts. By taking proactive steps to dispute inaccuracies and explore avenues for credit repair, individuals can begin to rebuild their financial standing and enhance their overall security.

Legal protections exist for Social Security beneficiaries facing debt collection. The Fair Debt Collection Practices Act provides guidelines to prevent harassment and abuse by debt collectors. Recipients of Social Security benefits must know that these funds are generally exempt from garnishment in most cases, which protects their income from being seized to pay off debts. Additionally, understanding the legal options available for disputing collection accounts can provide a sense of relief and control. Seniors and disabled individuals should utilize available resources to educate themselves about their rights, ensuring they are not taken advantage of during challenging financial times.

Financial counseling can be a valuable resource for seniors on Social Security who are struggling with credit issues. Many organizations offer free or low-cost counseling services that can help beneficiaries create a budget, manage debt, and develop strategies for improving their credit scores. These sessions can provide personalized guidance tailored to the unique needs of seniors and disabled individuals, who may face different financial challenges compared to the general population. By engaging with financial counselors, beneficiaries can gain confidence in managing their finances and creating a more secure financial future.

Building credit after experiencing a collection account is not impossible, and numerous resources are available to assist Social Security beneficiaries in this journey. Government programs and non-profit organizations often provide support in credit repair efforts. Programs may include financial education workshops, access to financial products designed for individuals with low credit scores, and advocacy services.

By leveraging these resources, seniors and disabled individuals can work towards improving their credit profiles, ultimately leading to enhanced financial security and a better quality of life.

Long-term Consequences of Unresolved Debt

Unresolved debt can lead to a myriad of long-term consequences that disproportionately affect seniors and disabled individuals receiving Social Security. When debts remain unpaid, creditors and debt collectors may take aggressive measures, which can include garnishing Social Security benefits, placing liens on property, or pursuing legal action. These actions not only pose a threat to financial stability but can also create significant emotional stress and anxiety. For many seniors, the thought of losing their limited income to cover debts can be overwhelming, leading to a decline in overall well-being and quality of life. The impact of unresolved debt extends beyond immediate financial concerns. Collection accounts can severely damage credit scores, making it challenging for individuals to secure loans or credit in the future.

For seniors and disabled persons, who may rely on credit for essential purchases or emergency expenses, a low credit score can limit financial options. Furthermore, a poor credit history can result in higher interest rates for any financing that is available, creating a cycle of debt that is difficult to escape. Understanding the long-term implications of carrying unresolved debt is crucial for making informed financial decisions.

Moreover, the presence of collection accounts can affect eligibility for certain government programs and benefits. Many assistance programs consider an applicant's financial standing, and unresolved debts can lead to disqualification or reduced benefits. For Social Security beneficiaries, this can mean losing access to vital resources that help maintain their quality of life. It is essential for seniors and disabled individuals to be aware of how their credit status may influence their eligibility for necessary support services and how they can protect their rights in these situations.

In addition to the financial ramifications, unresolved debt can have profound implications for mental health. The stress associated with constant communication from debt collectors, the fear of legal action, and the shame of financial hardship can lead to anxiety and depression. For seniors and disabled individuals, who may already face isolation and other health challenges, these emotional effects can be particularly detrimental. Seeking financial counseling and support can be a critical step in addressing both the financial and emotional aspects of debt, helping individuals regain control over their lives.

Fortunately, there are resources and strategies available for Social Security beneficiaries struggling with unresolved debt. Non-profit organizations often provide free or low-cost credit counseling services tailored to the needs of seniors and disabled persons. These organizations can assist in disputing inaccurate collection accounts, developing a budget, and exploring options for debt relief.

By taking proactive steps toward managing debt, individuals can mitigate the long-term consequences and work towards rebuilding their credit and financial stability, ultimately enhancing their quality of life.

Chapter 7: Resources for Free Credit Repair Services for Seniors

Identifying Legitimate Credit Repair Services

Identifying legitimate credit repair services is crucial for seniors and disabled persons receiving Social Security who are facing challenges with bad credit. The landscape of credit repair can be complex and, unfortunately, rife with scams that prey on vulnerable individuals. When seeking assistance, it is essential to look for services with a solid reputation, transparent practices, and a genuine commitment to helping clients understand their rights and options. Legitimate credit repair services should always offer a free initial consultation and provide clear information about their fees and services before any agreement is made.

A key indicator of a reputable credit repair service is its transparency regarding the process and expected outcomes. Legitimate organizations will explain how they plan to improve your credit, including the methods they will use to dispute inaccuracies on your credit report. They should also provide a realistic timeline for results, as credit repair typically does not yield immediate changes. Avoid services that promise to remove all negative items from your report or guarantee a specific score increase, as these claims are often misleading or impossible to fulfill.

Another important factor to consider is the certification and experience of the credit repair professionals. Look for services that employ certified credit counselors or those affiliated with reputable industry organizations. These professionals should be knowledgeable about the Fair Credit Reporting Act and other relevant laws that protect consumers, particularly Social Security beneficiaries. Their understanding of the legal framework is vital to ensuring that your rights are upheld throughout the credit repair process.

Furthermore, it is beneficial to seek out non-profit organizations that specialize in credit counseling for seniors and disabled persons. Many of these organizations offer free or low-cost services tailored to the unique financial situations faced by Social Security recipients. They can provide personalized financial counseling, help create a budget, and guide you through the process of disputing erroneous collection accounts. Utilizing such resources can not only help improve your credit but also provide you with valuable tools for managing your finances more effectively.

Lastly, always check for reviews and testimonials from previous clients before engaging with a credit repair service. Consumer feedback can provide insights into the quality of service and the success rates of the organization. Additionally, consulting with friends, family, or community groups can yield recommendations for reputable services. By conducting thorough research and remaining vigilant, you can identify legitimate credit repair services that will assist you in navigating the complexities of credit repair while protecting your rights as a Social Security beneficiary.

Government and Non-Profit Resources

Seniors and disabled persons receiving Social Security often face unique challenges when dealing with debt collectors, particularly when bad credit can exacerbate their financial situations. Fortunately, various government and non-profit resources are available to assist these individuals in asserting their rights and improving their financial health. Understanding these resources is crucial for navigating the complexities of debt collection and credit repair, ensuring that beneficiaries can access the support they need.

Government programs play a significant role in providing assistance to Social Security beneficiaries facing debt collection issues. The Federal Trade Commission (FTC) offers guidance on consumer rights, helping individuals understand the legal protections available to them under the Fair Debt Collection Practices Act. This federal law limits the actions of debt collectors, ensuring that they cannot engage in harassment or deceptive practices.

Additionally, the Consumer Financial Protection Bureau (CFPB) provides resources specifically tailored for seniors and disabled individuals, including information on how to dispute incorrect collection accounts and understand credit reports.

Non-profit organizations also serve as valuable allies for Social Security recipients struggling with debt. Many of these organizations offer free or low-cost financial counseling services that can help beneficiaries create budgets, manage debt, and develop effective credit repair strategies. For instance, the National Foundation for Credit Counseling (NFCC) partners with local agencies to provide personalized advice and education, empowering seniors and disabled persons to take control of their financial situations. These services often include workshops on credit management and one-on-one counseling sessions aimed at addressing specific financial concerns.

In addition to counseling, non-profit groups can help individuals take practical steps toward clearing their credit of collection accounts. Some organizations provide advocacy services, assisting individuals in disputing inaccurate entries on their credit reports. They also offer educational resources on how to negotiate with creditors effectively. For seniors, having access to knowledgeable advocates who understand the intricacies of credit reporting can be invaluable in achieving better outcomes when facing debt collection.

Overall, leveraging government and non-profit resources can significantly enhance the financial well-being of Social Security beneficiaries dealing with bad credit. By understanding their rights and utilizing available support systems, seniors and disabled persons can navigate the debt collection landscape more effectively. This not only aids in improving credit scores but also fosters a sense of empowerment, enabling individuals to build a more stable financial future despite past challenges.

How to Avoid Credit Repair Scams

Many seniors and disabled individuals receiving Social Security benefits face the challenge of managing their credit, particularly when dealing with collection accounts. Unfortunately, this vulnerability also makes them prime targets for credit repair scams. These scams often promise quick fixes for bad credit but can lead to more financial harm. To avoid falling victim, it is essential to recognize the red flags and understand the legitimate avenues available for credit repair.

One of the most significant warning signs of a credit repair scam is the demand for upfront payment. Legitimate credit repair organizations typically offer their services on a pay-as-you-go basis or only charge after the service is provided. If a company insists on full payment before any work has been done, it is advisable to proceed with caution. Additionally, be wary of any organization that guarantees results. Credit repair is a process that varies by individual circumstances, and no one can guarantee a specific outcome.

Another red flag is the use of high-pressure sales tactics. Reputable credit repair services will allow you to take your time to consider their offerings and will not rush you into a decision. If you feel pressured to sign a contract or make a payment immediately, it is a strong indicator that you should look elsewhere. Furthermore, be cautious of any company that instructs you to dispute legitimate debts or to create a new identity to avoid creditors, as these practices can lead to serious legal consequences.

It is crucial to educate yourself about your rights as a Social Security beneficiary, especially regarding debt collection. The Fair Debt Collection Practices Act provides specific protections against harassment and unfair practices by debt collectors. Understanding your rights can empower you to make informed choices when dealing with financial issues. Resources such as consumer protection agencies and legal aid organizations can provide valuable information and support, allowing you to navigate the complexities of credit repair without falling prey to scams.

Finally, consider leveraging non-profit organizations and government programs that offer free or low-cost financial counseling and credit repair services tailored for seniors and disabled individuals. These organizations can provide legitimate assistance without the risk of scams. They can help you develop strategies for disputing collection accounts, building your credit, and understanding the long-term impact of collection accounts on your Social Security benefits. By utilizing these resources, you can take proactive steps to improve your credit while safeguarding yourself against fraudulent schemes.

Chapter 8: Building Credit After a Collection Account for Social Security Beneficiaries

Steps to Rebuild Your Credit

To rebuild your credit, especially if you are a senior or a disabled person receiving Social Security, it is crucial to start by obtaining a copy of your credit report. You are entitled to one free report each year from each of the three major credit bureaus: Experian, TransUnion, and Equifax. Review your report carefully for any inaccuracies or outdated information, particularly regarding collection accounts. If you find discrepancies, you have the legal right to dispute these errors with the credit bureaus. Document your findings and provide any supporting evidence to strengthen your case. Correcting inaccuracies can significantly improve your credit score.

Next, focus on addressing any collection accounts listed on your credit report. If you have legitimate debts, consider negotiating with the debt collectors. Many collectors are willing to settle for less than the full amount owed, especially if you can offer a lump-sum payment. Be sure to get any settlement agreement in writing before making a payment. If the collection account is old, understand that it may not impact your credit as significantly as newer accounts. However, it is still essential to address it, as unpaid debts can lead to further legal complications.

Understanding your legal rights as a Social Security beneficiary is essential in navigating debt collection. The Fair Debt Collection Practices Act protects you from abusive practices by debt collectors. For instance, they cannot harass you or use deceptive tactics to collect debts. If you feel that a collector is violating your rights, you can file a complaint with the Consumer Financial Protection Bureau or seek legal assistance from organizations that specialize in consumer rights. Knowing these rights empowers you to take action against unfair treatment.

In addition to disputing accounts and negotiating debts, consider seeking financial counseling specifically designed for seniors on Social Security. Many non-profit organizations offer free or low-cost counseling services that can help you create a budget, manage your debts, and develop a plan to rebuild your credit. These services often provide personalized strategies tailored to your unique financial situation and can guide you towards using government programs that may assist with credit repair.

Lastly, building credit after dealing with collection accounts is a gradual process. Start by ensuring that your current bills are paid on time, as payment history significantly impacts your credit score. Consider applying for a secured credit card or a credit-builder loan, as these can help establish a positive credit history. Additionally, you can explore resources for free credit repair services available to seniors. By taking these proactive steps and utilizing available resources, you can improve your credit health and regain financial stability.

Secured Credit Cards and Their Benefits

Secured credit cards can be a valuable financial tool for seniors and disabled individuals receiving Social Security benefits, particularly those struggling with bad credit. Unlike traditional credit cards, secured credit cards require a cash deposit that serves as collateral, which typically becomes the card's credit limit. This arrangement minimizes risk for the lender, making secured cards more accessible for individuals with poor credit histories. For Social Security beneficiaries, this can be an opportunity to rebuild credit, improve financial standing, and create a more stable economic environment.

One of the primary benefits of secured credit cards is their potential to positively impact credit scores. By using the card responsibly—making purchases and paying the balance in full each month—users can demonstrate their reliability to creditors. Credit reporting agencies monitor these activities, and timely payments can lead to improved credit scores over time.

For seniors and disabled persons, this can be particularly beneficial, as a better credit score can facilitate access to other financial products and services, such as loans or housing options, that might have previously seemed out of reach.

Additionally, secured credit cards often come with features that can help users manage their finances. Many issuers provide online account management tools that allow cardholders to track spending, set budgets, and monitor their credit scores. This level of engagement is crucial for maintaining financial health, especially for those who may be new to managing credit or are recovering from past financial difficulties. By utilizing these tools, Social Security beneficiaries can gain greater control over their financial situations and make informed decisions about their spending habits.

Furthermore, some secured credit cards report to all three major credit bureaus, which can enhance the benefits of using such a card. Ensuring that credit activity is reported helps users establish a credit history that reflects their current financial behaviors rather than past mistakes.

This is especially important for seniors and disabled persons who may feel the long-term effects of past collection accounts. By actively working towards building a positive credit history, these individuals can increase their chances of qualifying for better financial products in the future.

Finally, the process of obtaining a secured credit card is generally straightforward and does not require a lengthy application process. Many banks and credit unions offer these cards with minimal eligibility requirements, making them accessible for those with limited credit histories. For Social Security beneficiaries, securing a card can be the first step in a larger strategy to clear their credit of collection accounts and improve their overall financial health. In conclusion, secured credit cards serve as a practical option for seniors and disabled persons seeking to rebuild their credit profiles while enjoying the benefits of responsible credit use.

Establishing Positive Credit History

Establishing a positive credit history is crucial for seniors and disabled individuals receiving Social Security, particularly if they have faced challenges with bad credit. A solid credit history not only opens doors to better loan terms and interest rates but also enhances overall financial security. To begin, it is essential to understand what constitutes a good credit history. This includes making timely payments on any debts, maintaining low credit card balances, and responsibly managing existing credit accounts. Even small, consistent actions can significantly impact credit scores over time, helping to create a more favorable financial profile.

One of the first steps in rebuilding credit is addressing any existing collection accounts. Social Security beneficiaries have specific rights under the Fair Debt Collection Practices Act, which protects them from harassment and unfair treatment by debt collectors. You can file disputes with the credit bureaus, providing evidence to support your case. This proactive approach can lead to the removal of erroneous entries, thus positively impacting your credit history and score.

In addition to disputing inaccuracies, it is vital to explore financial counseling services available to seniors on Social Security. Many non-profit organizations offer free or low-cost financial counseling tailored to the unique circumstances of seniors and disabled individuals. These services can help you create a manageable budget, understand your rights regarding debt collection, and develop a plan to improve your credit score. A counselor can also assist you in developing a strategy for paying off debts while balancing your everyday expenses.

Utilizing government programs designed to assist with credit repair can also be beneficial. Various local and federal initiatives provide resources and support for individuals looking to improve their credit. These programs often focus on educating participants about financial literacy, helping them navigate the complexities of credit scoring, and offering access to credit repair services. By taking advantage of these resources, Social Security beneficiaries can gain valuable insights and support in their journey towards rebuilding their credit history.

Lastly, it is essential to remain patient and persistent. Building a positive credit history takes time, but consistent efforts can yield significant results. Establishing new credit accounts, such as secured credit cards or installment loans, can help demonstrate responsible credit use. Always ensure that your payments are made on time and that you monitor your credit report regularly for any changes. By understanding your rights and leveraging available resources, you can effectively work towards a stronger credit history, enhancing your financial stability and overall quality of life.

Chapter 9: Using Government Programs to Assist with Credit Repair

Overview of Available Government Programs

Government programs designed to support seniors and disabled individuals receiving Social Security can play a pivotal role in addressing the challenges of bad credit and debt collection. These programs often provide financial assistance, legal guidance, and resources for credit repair. Understanding the range of available government initiatives can empower Social Security beneficiaries to take control of their financial situations and work towards improving their credit scores.

One significant government program is the Low-Income Home Energy Assistance Program (LIHEAP), which aids eligible seniors and disabled persons in managing their energy costs. By reducing utility bills, beneficiaries can allocate more of their limited income towards paying off debts or settling collection accounts.

Additionally, the Supplemental Nutrition Assistance Program (SNAP) can help alleviate food insecurity, allowing recipients to better manage their budgets and prioritize debt repayment without sacrificing essential needs.

Furthermore, the Social Security Administration (SSA) itself offers resources that can help beneficiaries navigate the complexities of debt collection. The SSA provides information on the legal protections available to Social Security recipients, including the fact that Social Security benefits are generally exempt from garnishment by debt collectors. These protections allow individuals to maintain a level of financial stability while they address their credit issues, ensuring that they have the necessary funds for daily living expenses.

In addition to direct financial assistance, various government-sponsored financial counseling programs are available specifically for seniors and individuals with disabilities. These programs can offer personalized strategies for disputing collection accounts, managing debt, and rebuilding credit.

By working with trained counselors, beneficiaries can develop actionable plans that take into account their unique financial situations and goals, ultimately empowering them to make informed decisions regarding their credit.

Finally, the collaboration between government programs and non-profit organizations can further enhance the support available to Social Security beneficiaries. Many non-profits provide free or low-cost credit repair services, financial education, and legal advocacy tailored to the needs of seniors and disabled persons. By leveraging these resources, beneficiaries can access a comprehensive network of support that addresses both their immediate credit concerns and their overall financial well-being, ensuring that they are equipped to face the challenges posed by debt collectors.

Eligibility Requirements

Eligibility requirements for protection against debt collectors are crucial for seniors and disabled persons receiving Social Security benefits. To qualify for these protections, individuals must first be recipients of Social Security income, which includes Social Security Disability Insurance (SSDI) and Supplemental Security Income (SSI). These benefits are designed to provide financial support to those who are unable to work due to age or disability. It is important for beneficiaries to understand that their income from Social Security is generally exempt from garnishment by debt collectors, providing them with a layer of security as they navigate their financial challenges.

Additionally, beneficiaries must be aware of the specific types of debts that are subject to collection. Certain debts, such as federal student loans or unpaid federal taxes, may have different rules regarding collection practices. However, most private debt, including medical bills or credit card debt, must comply with the Fair Debt Collection Practices Act (FDCPA).

This federal law restricts how debt collectors can interact with individuals, ensuring that they cannot harass or intimidate beneficiaries. Understanding the nuances of these protections can empower Social Security recipients to stand firm against inappropriate collection tactics.

Another critical aspect of eligibility revolves around the legal rights of Social Security beneficiaries in debt collection scenarios. Individuals have the right to dispute any inaccuracies on their credit reports, especially if those inaccuracies stem from illegitimate collection practices. By requesting validation of the debt, beneficiaries can ensure that they are not held accountable for erroneous claims. Furthermore, if a collection agency fails to provide adequate proof of the debt, beneficiaries may have grounds for legal recourse, allowing them to protect their credit standing and Social Security benefits. Financial counseling services tailored to seniors on Social Security can also play a significant role in understanding eligibility requirements. Many organizations offer free or low-cost financial counseling, specifically aimed at helping individuals manage their debts and improve their credit scores.

These services often include personalized advice on disputing collection accounts, budgeting, and accessing government programs designed to assist with credit repair. By leveraging these resources, beneficiaries can gain insights into their financial rights and responsibilities, ultimately enhancing their financial well-being.

Finally, it is essential to recognize the role of non-profit organizations that support Social Security recipients in navigating credit challenges. These organizations often provide educational workshops, one-on-one counseling, and resources aimed at improving financial literacy among seniors and disabled persons. They can assist in understanding the impact of collection accounts on Social Security benefits and guide beneficiaries through the process of rebuilding their credit after encountering debt. By connecting with these resources, individuals can equip themselves with the knowledge needed to advocate for their rights and achieve greater financial stability.

How to Apply for Assistance

When applying for assistance, it is essential to start by gathering all necessary documentation related to your Social Security benefits and your current financial situation. This includes your Social Security award letter, bank statements, credit reports, and any correspondence you have received from debt collectors. Having this information readily available will help you present a clear picture of your financial status to potential assistance programs or financial counselors. Remember that being organized not only streamlines the application process but also strengthens your case when seeking help.

Next, research local and national resources that specifically cater to seniors and disabled individuals receiving Social Security. Numerous organizations offer assistance programs designed to help with credit repair, financial counseling, and legal advice. Websites such as the National Council on Aging and local Area Agencies on Aging can provide valuable information about available resources.

Additionally, many non-profit organizations focus on advocating for the rights of Social Security beneficiaries, which can be a crucial ally in your quest for assistance.

Once you have identified suitable programs, reach out to them directly to inquire about their application processes. Many organizations offer free consultations that can help clarify your options. Be prepared to explain your situation in detail, including any debts you are facing and the impact they have on your Social Security benefits. This information will enable the program representatives to tailor their advice and support to your specific needs. It's also beneficial to ask about any eligibility requirements or documentation you may need to provide during the application process.

After you submit your application for assistance, it is crucial to follow up regularly. Many organizations may experience high volumes of applications, and a gentle reminder can help ensure your case receives the attention it deserves. Keep records of all communications, including dates and names of representatives you speak with.

This documentation can be invaluable if you need to escalate your case or seek additional support. Persistence is key, and demonstrating your commitment to resolving your financial situation can make a significant difference.

Lastly, consider combining your application for assistance with proactive measures to improve your credit status. Engage with financial counselors who specialize in helping Social Security beneficiaries, as they can offer practical strategies for disputing collection accounts and rebuilding your credit. Additionally, explore government programs designed to assist with credit repair and understand how non-profit organizations can further support your efforts. By taking a proactive approach, you not only increase your chances of receiving assistance but also empower yourself to regain control of your financial future.

Chapter 10: The Role of Non-Profit Organizations in Helping Social Security Recipients

Finding Non-Profit Organizations in Your Area

Finding non-profit organizations in your area can be a crucial step for seniors and disabled individuals receiving Social Security benefits who are dealing with bad credit. These organizations often provide essential services that can help you navigate the complexities of debt collection, improve your financial situation, and ultimately work towards repairing your credit. To begin your search, consider reaching out to local community centers, senior service organizations, or disability advocacy groups, as they may have established relationships with reputable non-profits that specialize in financial counseling and credit repair for vulnerable populations.

Another effective method for locating non-profit organizations is to utilize online resources. Websites such as the National Foundation for Credit Counseling and the United Way can guide you to local chapters and affiliated organizations that offer free or low-cost services tailored to your needs. Many of these non-profits provide workshops, one-on-one counseling, and educational materials focused on understanding your rights as a Social Security beneficiary and developing strategies to dispute collection accounts and improve your credit score. Being proactive in your search can yield a wealth of resources that are specifically designed to support you.

Once you identify potential non-profit organizations, it is important to research their credibility and the services they offer. Look for organizations that are accredited and have a solid reputation within your community. Additionally, consider reading testimonials from other seniors or disabled individuals who have benefited from their services. This can give you a better understanding of how these organizations operate and what you can expect when seeking help.

Many non-profits also offer specialized programs for Social Security recipients, ensuring that their services align with your unique circumstances.

Once you identify potential non-profit organizations, it is important to research their credibility and the services they offer. Look for organizations that are accredited and have a solid reputation within your community. Additionally, consider reading testimonials from other seniors or disabled individuals who have benefited from their services. This can give you a better understanding of how these organizations operate and what you can expect when seeking help. Many non-profits also offer specialized programs for Social Security recipients, ensuring that their services align with your unique circumstances.

In addition to credit repair services, some non-profit organizations may provide comprehensive financial counseling that includes budgeting assistance, debt management plans, and guidance on using government programs to aid in your credit repair efforts.

These programs can be particularly beneficial as they may help you develop a more sustainable financial plan, allowing you to regain control over your finances and improve your creditworthiness. Engaging with these organizations can empower you to take action and make informed decisions about your financial future.

Finally, it is essential to maintain ongoing communication with the non-profit organization you choose to work with. Regular check-ins can help you stay on track with your financial goals and ensure that you are making progress in disputing collection accounts or managing your debts. Additionally, staying informed about your rights as a Social Security beneficiary will enable you to advocate for yourself effectively. By leveraging the resources and support provided by non-profit organizations, you can take meaningful steps towards clearing your credit and achieving greater financial stability.

Services Offered by Non-Profits

Non-profit organizations play a crucial role in providing essential services to seniors and disabled individuals receiving Social Security benefits, especially for those facing challenges related to bad credit. These organizations often focus on financial education, credit repair, and advocacy, which are particularly valuable for individuals who may be unfamiliar with their rights and options in managing debt. By offering tailored resources and support, non-profits empower Social Security recipients to take control of their financial situations and navigate the complexities of debt collection.

One of the primary services offered by non-profits is financial counseling. Many organizations provide one-on-one sessions or group workshops aimed at educating seniors and disabled persons about budgeting, credit management, and debt repayment strategies.

These counseling sessions can help individuals understand their financial standing and develop actionable plans to improve their credit. Counselors often assist clients in creating realistic budgets that accommodate their Social Security income while addressing outstanding debts, ensuring that they can maintain their living expenses.

In addition to financial counseling, non-profits often assist with disputing collection accounts. They provide guidance on the legal rights of Social Security beneficiaries in the debt collection process, helping individuals understand their protections under the Fair Debt Collection Practices Act. Non-profit advocates can assist clients in drafting dispute letters to challenge inaccuracies on their credit reports, which may lead to the removal of erroneous collection accounts. This process is vital for individuals looking to clear their credit history and improve their overall financial health.

Non-profits also serve as a valuable resource for free credit repair services. Many organizations offer workshops or access to professionals who can provide insights into legitimate credit repair strategies.

These services may include instruction on how to assess credit reports, identify errors, and work through the dispute process. By utilizing these resources, Social Security beneficiaries can take proactive steps toward repairing their credit without incurring additional costs that may be challenging to manage on a limited income.

Finally, non-profit organizations frequently collaborate with government programs to enhance their services and provide comprehensive support for credit repair. These partnerships can lead to additional resources, such as grants or specialized programs tailored for low-income individuals. By leveraging these government initiatives, non-profits can expand their reach and effectiveness in assisting Social Security recipients. Ultimately, the combination of financial counseling, assistance with disputes, credit repair resources, and collaboration with government programs creates a robust support network for seniors and disabled persons striving to improve their financial circumstances.

Success Stories and Testimonials

Many seniors and disabled individuals receiving Social Security have faced the overwhelming burden of debt collection, often feeling trapped and unsure of their rights. However, numerous success stories illustrate that it is possible to navigate these challenges and achieve financial stability.

Case Study #1

For instance, take the case of Mary, a 70-year-old widow on Social Security who found herself struggling with a collection account that threatened her meager savings. Through diligent research and understanding her rights, Mary successfully disputed the collection, leading to its removal from her credit report. Her story serves as an inspiration to others facing similar situations, highlighting the importance of knowing one's rights and the potential for positive outcomes.

Case Study #2

Another compelling story comes from James, a disabled veteran who, after losing track of his finances, found himself overwhelmed with collection calls. Instead of succumbing to despair, he reached out to a local non-profit organization that specializes in helping seniors and disabled individuals with financial counseling. With their guidance, James learned effective strategies for disputing collection accounts and rebuilding his credit. Within a year, he was able to improve his credit score significantly, allowing him to secure a small loan for home repairs. His experience reinforces the message that seeking help and utilizing available resources can lead to remarkable transformations in financial health.

Case Study #3

The impact of understanding one's legal rights cannot be overstated, as evidenced by the journey of Linda, a Social Security beneficiary who felt powerless against aggressive debt collectors. After attending a workshop on legal protections for Social Security recipients, she learned about her rights under the Fair Debt Collection Practices Act. Empowered with this knowledge, Linda successfully challenged a collection agency that was attempting to seize her benefits. Her testimony emphasizes that awareness and education can empower individuals to stand up against unfair practices, making a significant difference in their lives.

Case Study #4

In addition to individual stories, many seniors have benefited from utilizing government programs designed to assist with credit repair. For example, Robert, a retired teacher, discovered a program that allowed him to access free credit counseling services. Through this program, he received personalized advice on managing his debts and improving his credit score. With consistent effort and the support of the program, Robert was able to clear his credit report of old collection accounts, restoring his financial dignity. This illustrates the vital role that government initiatives can play in helping seniors regain control over their financial futures.

Finally, the collective experiences of these individuals highlight the essential role of community support and non-profit organizations. Many seniors have shared how organizations dedicated to financial education and advocacy have provided them with the tools they need to succeed. These entities not only assist with disputing collection accounts but also offer workshops that teach valuable skills for budgeting and credit repair. By fostering a supportive environment, these organizations empower Social Security beneficiaries to reclaim their financial health and build a brighter future.

Chapter 11: Conclusion and Next Steps

Recap of Your Rights and Resources

Understanding your rights and available resources is crucial for seniors and disabled persons receiving Social Security, especially if you are facing challenges with bad credit. Social Security beneficiaries are afforded specific legal protections against debt collectors, recognizing the unique vulnerabilities associated with limited income and the potential impact of aggressive collection practices. Familiarizing yourself with these rights is the first step in safeguarding your financial well-being and ensuring that you do not face undue pressure from collectors who may not be aware of or choose to disregard the protections afforded to you.

When it comes to disputing collection accounts, Social Security recipients have the right to contest inaccuracies in their credit reports. If a debt collector is attempting to collect a debt that is not yours, or if the amount is incorrect, you can dispute the account with the credit bureaus. Under the Fair Debt Collection Practices Act, you can also request verification of the debt from the collector, and they are legally obligated to provide proof. Documenting your communications and maintaining records of your disputes is essential, as this evidence can support your claims if the issue escalates.

Moreover, it is important to recognize how collection accounts can affect your Social Security benefits. While the government cannot garnish your Social Security payments to pay off most debts, certain conditions may lead to deductions, such as for federal taxes or child support. Understanding these nuances can empower you to take proactive steps in managing your debts while protecting your essential income. Seeking financial counseling specifically tailored for seniors on Social Security can provide you with personalized strategies to navigate these challenges effectively.

Resources for free credit repair services are available for seniors and disabled individuals, often provided by non-profit organizations dedicated to financial education and support. These organizations can assist you in understanding your credit report, developing a budget, and creating a plan to improve your credit score. Many non-profits also offer workshops and one-on-one counseling sessions, which can be invaluable for those looking to regain control over their financial situation after experiencing collection accounts.

Lastly, utilizing government programs designed to assist with credit repair can further bolster your efforts. Programs may offer assistance with negotiating debts or provide access to financial literacy resources. By taking advantage of these services, you can build credit after a collection account more effectively, ensuring a brighter financial future. Being informed about your rights and the resources available to you is not just empowering; it is a vital step towards reclaiming your financial independence and peace of mind.

Taking Action: Empowering Yourself

Taking action to empower yourself as a Social Security beneficiary can lead to significant improvements in your financial situation, especially if you are struggling with bad credit due to collection accounts. Understanding your rights under the Fair Debt Collection Practices Act is crucial. This law protects you from abusive debt collection tactics, ensuring that you are treated fairly. If you receive a collection notice, remember that you have the right to dispute the debt. Gather all relevant documents, including any communication from the collector, and respond within the specified time frame. By asserting your rights, you take the first step in regaining control over your financial health.

Disputing collection accounts can be an effective strategy for clearing your credit. Start by checking your credit report for inaccuracies; you are entitled to one free report per year from each of the three major credit bureaus.

If you find errors, draft a dispute letter outlining the inaccuracies and include documentation that supports your claim. Send this letter via certified mail to ensure it is received. After your dispute is filed, the credit bureau must investigate and respond within 30 days. This process not only helps clear your credit history but also reinforces your position as an informed and proactive consumer.

Understanding the legal rights afforded to you as a Social Security beneficiary in the face of debt collection is vital. Your benefits are typically protected from garnishment for most debts, which means that collectors cannot take your Social Security payments to satisfy debts. However, it's important to understand the exceptions, such as for federal tax debts or child support. Knowing these nuances can empower you to better navigate your financial challenges. If you feel your rights are being violated, consider contacting a legal aid organization that specializes in consumer rights for guidance.

Financial counseling can also play a significant role in empowering you. Many non-profit organizations offer free or low-cost financial counseling specifically tailored for seniors and individuals with disabilities. These services can help you create a budget, manage debt, and develop a plan for rebuilding your credit. Counselors can also assist you in understanding how collection accounts impact your Social Security benefits and provide strategies to mitigate those effects. Engaging with a counselor not only provides practical advice but can also offer emotional support during a challenging time.

Finally, take advantage of government programs and resources designed to assist with credit repair. Various initiatives provide educational resources, workshops, and even direct assistance in managing debts and improving credit scores. Non-profit organizations often collaborate with these programs to offer comprehensive support tailored to your needs as a Social Security beneficiary. By leveraging these resources, you can build a stronger financial foundation, reduce anxiety related to credit issues, and ultimately empower yourself to achieve greater financial stability.

Staying Informed and Seeking Support

Staying informed about your rights and available resources is crucial for seniors and disabled persons receiving Social Security, especially when dealing with the stress of bad credit and debt collection. Knowledge of your legal protections can empower you to take action against unfair practices by debt collectors. The Fair Debt Collection Practices Act provides specific rights to consumers, including Social Security beneficiaries. These rights include the ability to dispute inaccuracies on your credit report and to request validation of debts. Understanding these protections can help you navigate the often overwhelming landscape of debt collection.

When faced with collection accounts, it is essential to develop effective strategies for disputing inaccuracies that may affect your credit score. Begin by obtaining a copy of your credit report from the three major credit bureaus. Review the report carefully for any errors or unfamiliar accounts.

If you identify any discrepancies, you can file a dispute with the credit bureau, providing necessary documentation to support your claim. Be sure to keep records of all correspondence. This proactive approach can help clear your credit of collection accounts and prevent further negative impacts on your Social Security benefits.

Seniors and disabled persons must be aware of their legal rights when dealing with debt collectors. For instance, Social Security benefits cannot be garnished to pay off most types of debts. Additionally, collectors are prohibited from harassing or threatening you. Familiarizing yourself with these rights can build your confidence when communicating with debt collectors. If you feel your rights have been violated, consider reaching out to a legal aid organization for assistance. They can help you understand your options and may provide representation if necessary.

Financial counseling can be an invaluable resource for seniors on Social Security. Many organizations offer free or low-cost financial counseling services specifically tailored to your needs.

These counselors can help you create a budget, manage debt, and improve your overall financial health. They may also provide advice on building credit after dealing with collection accounts. Engaging with a financial counselor can equip you with the tools and knowledge to regain control of your finances while ensuring that your Social Security benefits remain protected.

In addition to financial counseling, various government programs and non-profit organizations exist to assist Social Security recipients with credit repair. These resources can guide you on the best practices for managing your credit and navigating the complexities of debt collection. Many non-profit organizations focus on helping seniors and disabled persons understand their rights and access support services. By utilizing these resources, you can take proactive steps toward improving your financial situation and ensuring that you receive the full benefits you are entitled to while also working toward a healthier credit profile.

Disclaimer:

The information contained in this book, "KNOW YOUR RIGHTS: LEGAL PROTECTIONS FOR SOCIAL SECURITY BENEFICIARIES AGAINST DEBT COLLECTORS," is intended for general informational purposes only.

It is not, and should not be construed as, legal advice on any matter. Readers are advised that the content of this book is based on laws, regulations, and practices that are subject to change from state to state. While every effort has been made to ensure the accuracy and completeness of the information provided, the author and publisher make no warranties or representations regarding the currency, suitability, or applicability of the content for any specific legal situation.

Seek Professional Advice: Readers are strongly encouraged to consult with a qualified attorney or legal professional to obtain advice tailored to their particular circumstances. Legal issues are often complex and vary greatly depending on individual facts and jurisdiction. Only a licensed attorney can provide legal advice that takes into account the specific context and nuances of a reader's situation.

No Attorney-Client Relationship: The use of this book does not create an attorney-client relationship between the reader and the author, publisher, or any legal professionals referenced within the content. An attorney-client relationship is only established through direct, personal contact with a licensed attorney, and upon the execution of a written agreement for legal services.

Liability Disclaimer: The author and publisher disclaim any and all liability for any loss, damage, or inconvenience arising, directly or indirectly, from the use or reliance on the information provided in this book. This includes, but is not limited to, legal, financial, or other consequences that may arise from errors, omissions, or inaccuracies in the content.

Jurisdictional Variations: Laws and regulations governing debt collection and legal protections for Social Security beneficiaries can vary significantly between jurisdictions. Readers should be aware that the information provided in this book may not be applicable in all locations and should verify the legal requirements in their specific area.

Acknowledgment: By using this book, readers acknowledge that they have read and understood this disclaimer and agree to seek professional legal advice when necessary. The author and publisher reiterate the importance of consulting with a qualified attorney to address any legal issues or concerns.

Know Your Rights: Legal Protections for Social Security Beneficiaries Against Debt Collectors

The book delves into federal and state regulations designed to safeguard the financial well-being of those receiving Social Security benefits, including detailed explanations of the Fair Debt Collection Practices Act (FDCPA) and other relevant laws. Readers will learn how to recognize unlawful debt collection tactics, assert their rights effectively, and take necessary steps to clear their credit.

www.ingramcontent.com/pod-product-compliance
Lightning Source LLC
LaVergne TN
LVHW022103200926
848481LV00003B/1055
* 9 7 9 8 2 2 7 2 3 4 1 2 4 *